Heirloom Quilt Designs for Today

Lori Martin

Schiffer Publishing Ltd
4880 Lower Valley Road, Atglen, Pennsylvania 19310 USA

Other Schiffer Books on Related Subjects
Amish Arts of Lancaster County. Patricia T. Herr.
Amish Quilts of Lancaster County. Patricia T. Herr.
Fiber Expressions: The Contemporary Quilt. Quilt National.
The History of the Patchwork Quilt. Schnuppe von Gwinner.
Menonite Arts. Clarke Hess.
New Quilts. Nancy Rae.
Pennsylvania German Arts: More Than Hearts, Parrots, & Tulips. Irwin Richman.
A People and Their Quilts. John Rice Irwin.
The Quilt: New Directions for an American Tradition. Quilt National.
Quilting Traditions: Pieces from the Past. Patricia T. Herr.
Quilts and Quiltmakers Covering Connecticut. The Connecticut Quilt Search Project.
Quilts of Virginia 1607-1899: The Birth of America Through the Eye of a Needle. Virginia Consortium of Quilters' Documentation Project.
Quilts: The Fabric of Friendship. The York County Quilt Documentation Project & The York County Heritage Trust.
Ralli Quilts: Traditional Textiles from Pakistan and India. Patricia Ormsby Stoddard.

Disclaimer

The information presented in this text is based on the author's personal knowledge of quilts and quilting, which has been gathered over many years while working with and interviewing other quilters.

Library of Congress Control Number: 2006938894

Designed by "Sue"
Galliard BT/Aldine 721 BT

ISBN: 978-0-7643-2669-1
Printed in China

Published by Schiffer Publishing Ltd.
4880 Lower Valley Road
Atglen, PA 19310
Phone: (610) 593-1777; Fax: (610) 593-2002
E-mail: Info@schifferbooks.com

For the largest selection of fine reference books on this and related subjects, please visit our web site at **www.schiffer-books.com**
We are always looking for people to write books on new and related subjects. If you have an idea for a book please contact us at the above address.

This book may be purchased from the publisher.
Include $3.95 for shipping.
Please try your bookstore first.
You may write for a free catalog.

In Europe, Schiffer books are distributed by
Bushwood Books
6 Marksbury Ave.
Kew Gardens
Surrey TW9 4JF England
Phone: 44 (0) 20 8392-8585; Fax: 44 (0) 20 8392-9876
E-mail: info@bushwoodbooks.co.uk
Website: www.bushwoodbooks.co.uk
Free postage in the U.K., Europe; air mail at cost.

Contents

Introduction: About Lori Martin

As a young child I loved to go to sewing circles and quilting bees with my mother. To see the designs come to life as they were being quilted was always fascinating to me. Of course I spent a lot of time under the quilt frame watching the needles come down and return up, watching the thread and scissors being passed over the quilt from quilter to quilter. All of this seemed very synchronized to me. Always having a quilt on my bed I remember tracing the blocks with my fingers before going to sleep. When I was twelve years old, my mother and I made a quilt for my bed. I was so excited to be able to pick out the fabrics, and then decorate my room around the quilt. The pattern was the snowball and I knew it was the most beautiful quilt ever made. Family and friends help us quilt it and, by the time the first snowflake fell, my snowball quilt was proudly on my bed.

Twenty years ago I took a job in a local quilt shop. I knew I loved quilts and had some experience making them. Both of my grandmothers were avid quilters and I had lots of family that were quilters. What I didn't know then was that this job would launch a passion for quilts and a career selling and commissioning them.

In the last ten years I have been fortunate to be able to work closely with a group of over 100 quilters that provide quilts and quilt-related items for Village Quilts at Kitchen Kettle Village. When we opened Village Quilts we decided we would specialize in hand quilted heirloom quilts. The best way to ensure such quality was to commission the quilters, so I work closely with each quilter researching patterns, creating new designs, and selecting our first quality cotton fabrics and quilting supplies.

The longer I am in the quilt business, the more personal it has become. I find myself wanting to do more to preserve the original art of hand quilting and also the culture from which it originates.

As our world has become fast-paced and extremely competitive, there is a peace, satisfaction, and value that come with taking the time to make a craft with your hands. For those who do care about the art, the artist, and about preserving and having heirloom's for the future, we quilters want to continue providing our quilts.

With the influx of imported quilts showing up even right here in the quilting capital of America, I realize that even this art can be imitated, as so many other arts already have been. I want to do my part to both ensure that quilt collectors may still find hand quilted quilts and my talented artist continue to have a place to proudly sell their art.

Special Thanks

To all my many quilters, who work very hard to do their best and to meticulously work on each project. Without each of you, this book could not have been completed. A special thanks to my sales staff at Village Quilts and to Jim Burnley of Burnley Enterprises for supporting and encouraging me through this process. To Pete Schiffer, at Schiffer Publishing, for being my patient editor.

I also want to thank my daughter Ashley for always being my source of inspiration and to my friend Bruce for being my sounding board and best critic. May God bless each one of you in a very special way.

Village Quilts

Detail from the quilting work on a Baskets quilt.

Based in Lancaster County, it is easy to see how our quilts resemble traditional Amish and Mennonite patterns. From the basic repetitive block and chain patterns, which make up a lot of our pieced patterns, to floral appliqué, set up other in block form or more recently using wide width fabrics to create more of a open canvas to appliqué on. Even though the look of the pattern and the colors used may change to keep pace with the contemporary styles and decor, the basic patterns really remain the same. As you view the quilts displayed here, notice how alterations in color, pattern, style, and visual texture play a large role in change the look of the same pattern on different quilts. What one person might think of as a traditional pattern can be altered to fit almost any decor.

Hand Quilting

To me, hand quilting is a under appreciated art form. Although the fabrics and the patterns make the foundation for the quilt, the hand quilting is what brings any quilt top to life. After working with my quilters for years, I can quickly identify the quilter by the quilting. It is like recognizing someone's handwriting. Each quilter's work has a recognizable look, just like a painter's.

Log Cabin Quilts

This pattern is a Lancaster County original and is probably one of the most recognized patterns among old fashioned quilts. There are many ways to manipulate this pattern to create a variety of different looks. The barn raising log cabin is probably the most recognizable Log Cabin set up and has been used in Lancaster County for many generations.

There are quite a few stories out there about how the Log Cabin pattern was named and the meaning behind this enduring pattern. One of my favorites explanations of the pattern's meaning is: "In life you will have good times which are represented by the light logs and you will have bad times, represented by the dark colored logs. But, if you have a solid center in God, your life will be fulfilling and balanced."

Using this traditional pattern and making some variations, it is amazing all the different patterns that can be made.

Log Cabin Amish Traditional Barn Raising Created with solid fabrics and hand quilted in black thread, it is set up in a barn raising variation with the dark and light side being very evident.

Log Cabin Barn Raising
Country classic fabrics and a traditional design make a popular creation with a burgundy, navy, green, and tan color scheme.

Log Cabin Barn Raising
An adaptation of the traditional Barn Raising log cabin design, this quilt is set up using a multitude of printed pastels fabrics.

Cornerstone Log Cabin
This is a combination of the Nine Patch and log cabin. Choice in color can change the look of this pattern drastically.

Cornerstone Log Cabin
This wall hanging made in shades of burgundy, navy, and tan has a primitive country feel.

Christmas Windows
A Christmas quilt of sage, green, red, and gold highlighted with a Christmas tree is a good example of how quilts have been used as pieces of textile art.

Log Cabin
A modern set up to an old traditional pattern. Due to the use of set up and fabric design, this pattern creates a spiral design.

Pineapple wall hanging
This pattern is a variation of the traditional Log Cabin, highlighted in classic country colors.

Pineapple
This is one of the many patterns that have been derived from the Log Cabin pattern; the piecing process for this quilt design is intricate due to the many small interlocking pieces. This quilt is a combination of three complimentary colors, all accentuating the floral print of the border.

When I look at this pattern it reminds me of one of my quilters, Mabel. Mabel died a few years ago; she was such a special quilter. I am sure she's still quilting in heaven. It is interesting how a quilt can invoke so much emotion. I can never look at a quilt pattern that she made for me and not recall all the interesting things she has taught me about quilting … and even more about the value of life.

Baskets

The Basket pattern has been used in Amish quilts for many years. There have been many variations of the Basket pattern. Whether made in the traditional style with solid fabrics and quilted with black thread or in more contemporary styles, the Basket pattern is always attractive.

Baskets: Amish Traditional

This a classic Amish Traditional pattern; years ago they used fabrics from old worn out gowns and dresses or leftover remnants from clothing making to produce quilts. I am sure if you were a mother that was using your daughters old dress fabrics to make a quilt like this one, that quilt would become a very special and sentimental item to have in her collection. Many Basket quilts made in Lancaster County in the 1930s were made from feed sacks, and others were made with small Calico prints.

It is amazing how color and fabric prints can change the whole look of the quilt.

Baskets Amish Traditional
This classic Amish traditional pattern is set on black fabric, with many colorful traditional

Baskets
An adaptation of the traditional Basket design, this quilt is set up using a multitude of printed pastels fabrics.

Postage Stamp Basket
The Postage Stamp Basket quilt is another beautiful variation of the Basket design. It got its name because the tops of all the baskets are made up of small blocks, each block the size of a postage stamp. This is a charming country quilt made of multiple calico prints.

Baskets
This wall hanging is comprised of different shades of green baskets on a cream background. This is a country classic.

Basket Sampler
This is a great wall hanging for all basket quilt collectors. It has a great selection of different baskets. From a basic pieced basket to a hand appliquéd basket, each one is a timeless treasure in the quilt community.

Pieced Patterns

Many pieced patterns have derived from older traditional patterns. Some quilters love the mathematical challenge that comes when you start to change and enhance old patterns to make a new look. In this section are examples of their resulting quilts.

Irish Chain

Double Irish Chain
This Amish traditional pattern has been adapted to highlight printed fabrics. With blue and white colors, it is a timeless classic.

Double Irish Chain
Traditional chain and block quilt highlighted with chocolate brown and crimson red, the contrasting hand quilting is one of the unique aspects of this creation.

Triple Irish Chain
This is another traditional Amish quilt pattern that has been adapted in many ways over the years. It is fun to see how trends affect quilt patterns. The use of homespun plaids makes this quilt unique and identifiable to the quilter. Years ago, scrap quilts were very popular; they were made out of actual scraps left over from other projects or clothing making. The scraps were used, not because they matched, but because we "Lancaster Countians" were taught to "waste not, want not."

In past years, as interior decoration moved toward continuous color themes and everything had to match, scrap quilts became "outdated". Now, with our renewed faith in family and memories, scrap quilts are regaining their popularity.

Barn Raising Log Cabin
Using rose, cream, and blue colors, this popular pattern is enhanced by beautiful floral fabric. Other examples of Log Cabin quilts may be found on pages 7 to 9.

A curvy Log Cabin
A modern take of a traditional pattern: manipulating the size of the patches, this design appears to have curves. It is made of classic country fabrics bordered with a black fabric.

Double Wedding Ring
An Amish traditional pattern accented with many different shades of autumn colors, leaving the decorator's accent pallet open to many choices.

Double Wedding Ring
This popular Amish traditional pattern is done in burgundy and green.

Double Wedding Ring
This Amish traditional pattern has been updated with classic blue and white fabrics and a toile backing.

Close up of the Double Wedding Ring

Railroad Crossing

Railroad Crossing
The use of colonial classic fabrics in this traditional Amish quilting pattern can be adapted to a wide range of interior designs due to the color flow and set up. I love that you can use so many different fabrics. And each one looks so different due to the fabric selection. It also shows the influence of modern technology on the traditional Amish quilting designs.

Close Up of Railroad Crossing
The use of contrasting quilting enhances the hand quilting patterns, here using white thread on navy fabric.

Railroad Crossing
This Amish traditional pattern, transformed by its Civil War reproduction fabrics, is a cherished member of the Tony and Marsha Smith quilt collection.

Railroad Crossing
This Amish traditional quilt has been updated with bright pastel color combinations.

Mariner's Compass

Mariner's Compass
Intricate patchwork is accented by the choice of soft cottage fabrics.

Close up of Mariner's Compass corner patch.

Mariner's Compass
This twenty-point compass made in shades of green is a challenge to any quilter and a beautiful addition to any room.

Moon Glow

Moon Glo
Based on the combination of the Mariner's Compass and Cornerstone Log Cabin quilt designs, the Moon Glo shows the complexity in piecing as well as incredible use of color. This example is machine pieced and hand quilted.

What an electrifying piece of art. Some quilts just need to be hung on a wall rather than spread on a bed. This piece is being proudly hung in a foyer at the Razukiewicz home in New York.

Clcse Up of Moon Glo
Variation of a Compass pattern, colors highlighting different aspects of the compass.

Close Up of Moon Glo

Pinwheel and Variations

Pinwheel Flowers
Another example of an old pattern set in a new pictorial style depicting a sunny day with sunflowers and grass. What a happy quilt for a child's room.

Wheel of Mystery
A modern rendition of a traditional Pinwheel, this quilt has a country French deco feel to it. All those angles can make this a challenging pattern. All of these angles are needed to form the underlying circular pattern.

Pinwheel
Pinwheel is a traditional quilt pattern and is often used in conjunction with another pattern. I love the use of the autumn colored batik fabrics shown here. This is a good example of how an old pattern can be adapted with modern fabrics.

Bars and Pinwheels
This pattern is made of hand dyed and printed African fabrics. When you begin to explore the fabric world, one of the first things you realize is that, while we think we have a lot of fabric in Lancaster County, there are fabrics made all over the world that are amazing pieces of cloth. This piece was made with hand dyed and hand stamped fabric made in Africa. The quilter highlighted the fabric by using a local traditional pattern, the Pinwheel and Amish Bars.

Stack & Whack
This kaleidoscope effect is created by using mirror geometry and quilting. It is amazing how many different looks you can create based on one fabric.

Kaleidoscope from the Stack and Whack.

Variation of the Kaleidoscope used in the Stack and Whack.

Fabric swatch that was used to make the kaleidoscope in the Stack and Whack.

Shoofly

Shoofly
This old Lancaster County pattern, sometimes called Hole in the Barn Door, is quilted in red, black, and gold. It is a great example of how color determined the accent patch. Each patch is made in the same method, but the color placement determined their characteristics.

Shoofly
A great example of a country quilt made with scrappy plaid fabrics with a cream border.

Churn Dash
A variation of a Shoofly, constructed in Civil War reproduction fabrics.

New Modern Designs

As quilting has become a nationally recognized art form, artist who were working in other mediums have moved to textile arts. This has created new, modern forms, quilt patterns and ideas that have opened the quilt world to a new canvas of artistic impression. Still, much of the basis for these modern creations remains rooted in the traditional Amish quilting patterns and designs.

Bargello/Modern Quilt

Bargello Spray
This brilliant textile hanging is made with hand dyed fabrics in rainbow hues of batiks. The spray of appliqué softens the sharp lines of the Bargello pattern.

Bargello Peak
Another way to set up the Bargello pattern, accenting the peaks comprised of autumn colors framed by a burnt orange border.

Bargello
As quilt patterns have evolved, patterns such as this Bargello have become new territory for our adventurous quilt artists. This Bargello with highlighted peaks and waves, exemplifies movement and color.

Color Wash Trip

Trip Around the World
This one-of-a-kind Trip Around the World is made of hand dyed fabrics set up in a color-wash style. Its bold and daring colors will demand attention in any room.

Close up of the Trip Around the World quilt.

Signature swatch of the Trip Around the World quilt.

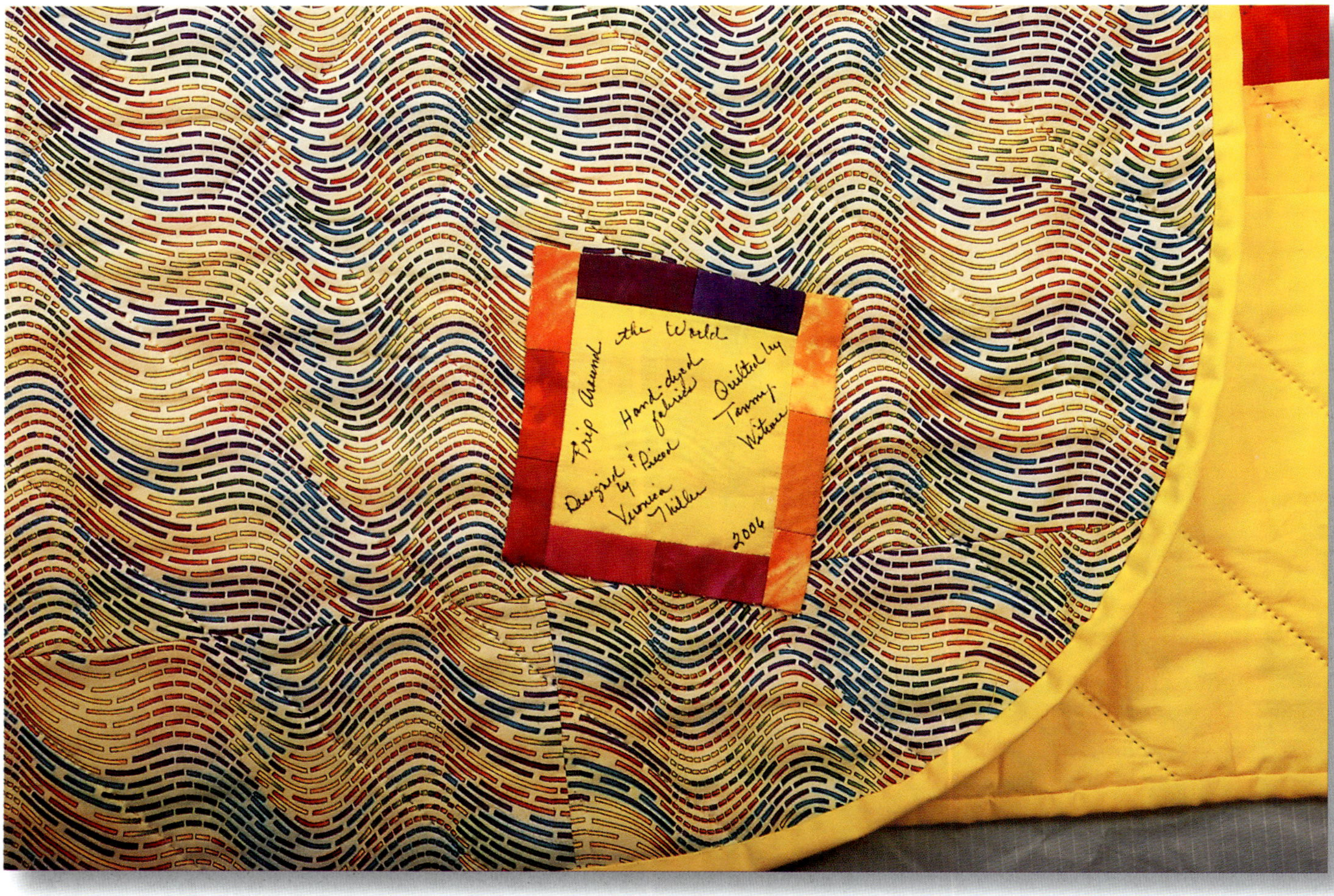
Trip Around the World
Hand-dyed fabrics
Quilted by
Designed & Pieced by
2006

Stained Glass Windows

Stained Glass Windows
This quilt is a modern take on a traditional Log Cabin, designed to mimic the subtle elegance of a stained glass window.

Close up of Stained Glass Windows quilt.

Variations on Amish Lone Star

Stars Over the Sea
Showing the majesty of two color quilts, this pattern is full of movement and rarely will be called boring.

Stars Over the Sea
Complex two-color quilt, this style would have been very popular in the late 1800s. Rooted in the traditional Star pattern, this color combination and set up creates an optical illusion.

Star in Commons
Great things happen when you start combining your favorite patterns. This quilt is a combination of three different quilts. The Amish Eight Point Star, the Center Diamond, and the Boston Commons patterns have become favorites of many visiting Lancaster County. The stars that highlight the pillow area are among its unique features.

Close up of Star In Commons quilt in navy, rose, and cream.

Backing of Star and Commons quilt, large floral fabric.

Signature corner of the Star and Commons quilt.

Star and Nine Patch
A combination of two traditional Amish patterns, the Nine Point Star and the Nine Patch, accented in homespun fabrics, creates a soft country feel.

Feathered Star
Derived from a traditional Lone Star pattern, this quilt's small pieces compliment the large printed floral fabric. The use of high contrasting burgundy, black, sage green, and tan colors, and detailed hand quilting makes this wall hanging a striking example of textile art.

Shadow Star
This pieced navy, burgundy, green, and tan quilt is a beautiful example of the Shadow Star design.

Shadow Star
This is a complicated quilt with rings comprised of a star set on a hexagon shape. An illusion of curves is created by the shadowing effect, which enhances the surrounding patchwork. Fall floral fabrics accented with greens, tans, and purples were used. The Shadow Star is definitely not a pattern I would start out a new "piecer" on.

The more you study this pattern, the more it has to say. Which is more powerful, the use of color to make the shadowing or the pattern itself? I don't know, but each one comes out a little differently and that is what makes them so unique.

Evening Star
A unique Block and Chain style quilt made of blues and creams.

Young Man's Fancy
This Block and Chain quilt, in aqua, blue, and white, use accent fabrics that have been set up to give it a unique design.

Theme Quilts

Christmas Patchwork
Highlighted with Christmas themed fabric, this quilt can be used for holiday decoration.

Bear Country
A combination of Patchwork and embroidery creates this themed quilt. Years ago many quilts had embroidery work in them. This themed crib quilt is a great way to decorate a nursery.

Planes
This themed quilt pattern has been known to make little boys smile. It may be made with many different primary colors and airplane designs.

Opposite page:
Bird In Hand Sampler
This country cottage themed wall hanging is a new idea that a few fabric companies have picked up on. They are printing themed fabric and motifs to make quilts with. This piece is beautifully accented with coordinating fabrics and lots of hand quilting.

Chinese Vases
This is a stunning Oriental themed wall hanging. Textile art is a great way to decorate your home; quilts are no longer just for the bedroom. This quilt would look great anywhere, from a dining room to a formal living room.

Falling Leaves
Derived from the traditional Maple Leaf pattern, we have chosen to update this pattern by selecting leaf-patterned fabric for the leaves and changing the background fabrics to look like the earth. The quilter has over eighty different leaf fabrics represented in her quilt. Each leaf is made up of different leaf fabrics. This pattern gives the feeling of such this beautiful time of year, with the crisp cool air and the brilliant colors of the leaves as they fall to the ground.

Center Diamond

This Amish Center Diamond example is a reproduction of an Amish traditional quilt that would have been seen in the mid- to late 1800s. It is made of new dress grade Batiste wool. Years ago most quilts were made of wool for a few different reasons. One reason was, quilts were usually made from leftover fabrics or recycled clothes. The second reason was that they did not have climate-controlled homes, so it was very important to make the quilts as warm as possible. Mary has been making traditional quilts for over fifty years. We have grown to love to research, and trace quilts to different Plain communities and families. We do our best to use colors that are as close to the original hand-dyed colors as possible and to ensure that our quilting patterns are the same. Mary is a remarkable Amish woman and I cherish all the things she has taught me about her quilts.

Center Diamond
An Amish traditional pattern comprised of black and turquoise with a purple center. This quilt is made of antique wools that were recycled from clothing and usually range between 80-100 years old.

Center Diamond
Amish traditional quilt made from new batiste wool fabric in black and cream with a burgundy center.

Amish Traditional Center Diamond
An antique reproduction from the early 1900s made of solid batiste wool hand quilted with black thread, this wall hanging is easily recognizable as a Lancaster County quilt.

Close up of Amish traditional wool center diamond.

Other Amish Traditional Patterns

Amish Triangles
An Amish traditional pattern made up with many different solid colors, highlighted with a burgundy and black border.

Opposite page:
Amish T
One of the more unusual Amish traditional patterns, this quilt is made of solid fabrics with a cream and black background.

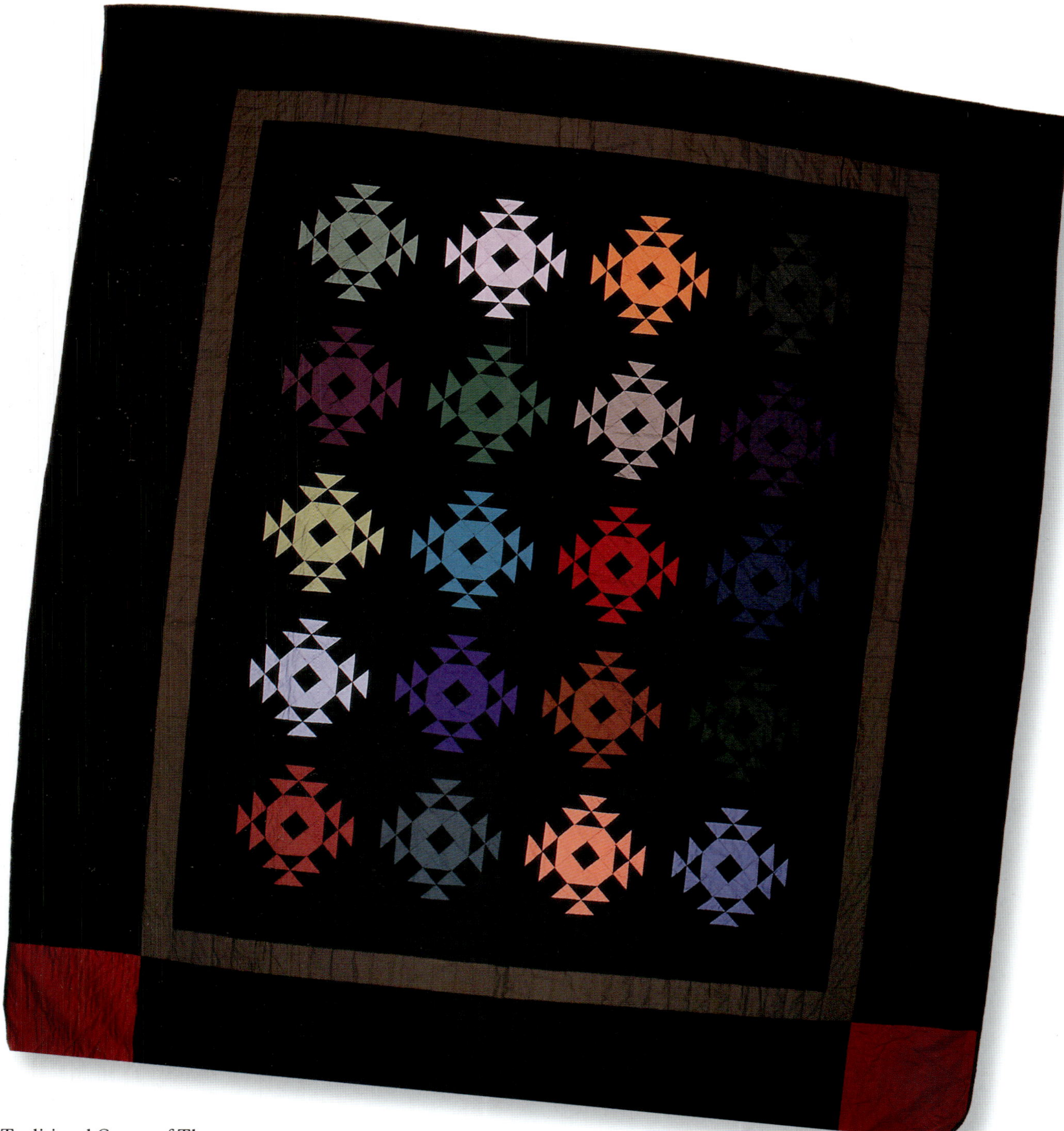

Traditional Crown of Thorns
This is a traditional Amish pattern. Elegant, bold, and artsy may all be words used to describe this piece in the art world. But to the thrifty Amish quilter, it is a good way to use up scraps from family clothes making.

Pyramiding Tumbling Blocks
Using a well-trained eye and a great deal of patience, it is amazing what one can do with solid fabrics.

Close up of Pyramiding Tumbling Blocks.

Nine Patch

There is nothing like the intensity of traditional Amish quilts. Double Nine Patch is a great demonstration in color, design, and intensity. I am always amazed how colors from both sides of the color wheel are easily blended when you look at a traditional piece. Years ago there were no color boundaries and that is one of the reasons for these remarkable blends. Today we are very quick to use cools, warms or neutrals, and not think of crossing over.

Amish traditional quilts stand out on their own as remarkable pieces of art. The Amish traditional Double Nine Patch is historically a pattern traced back to Lancaster County. This pattern was visible in this area in the early 1800s. It is a pattern that a lot of Amish woman would choose because you could use a lot of fabrics from you rag bag or scraps left over from making your family's clothing. Since most fabrics were hand dyed at that point, a wide variety in color is shown. Due to different grades in raw fabrics, water content, and dyeing skills, each piece that was colored would have a shade all its own. Different stories are told about the origin of the Double Nine's name. One story is that at the time when the ladies first made this pattern there were only nine Amish settlements. Another story is that if you made a bed size quilt with this pattern you would have nine whole patches, which included nine of the nine patches in each whole patch. Whichever is true, this pattern does make a beautiful Amish traditional quilt.

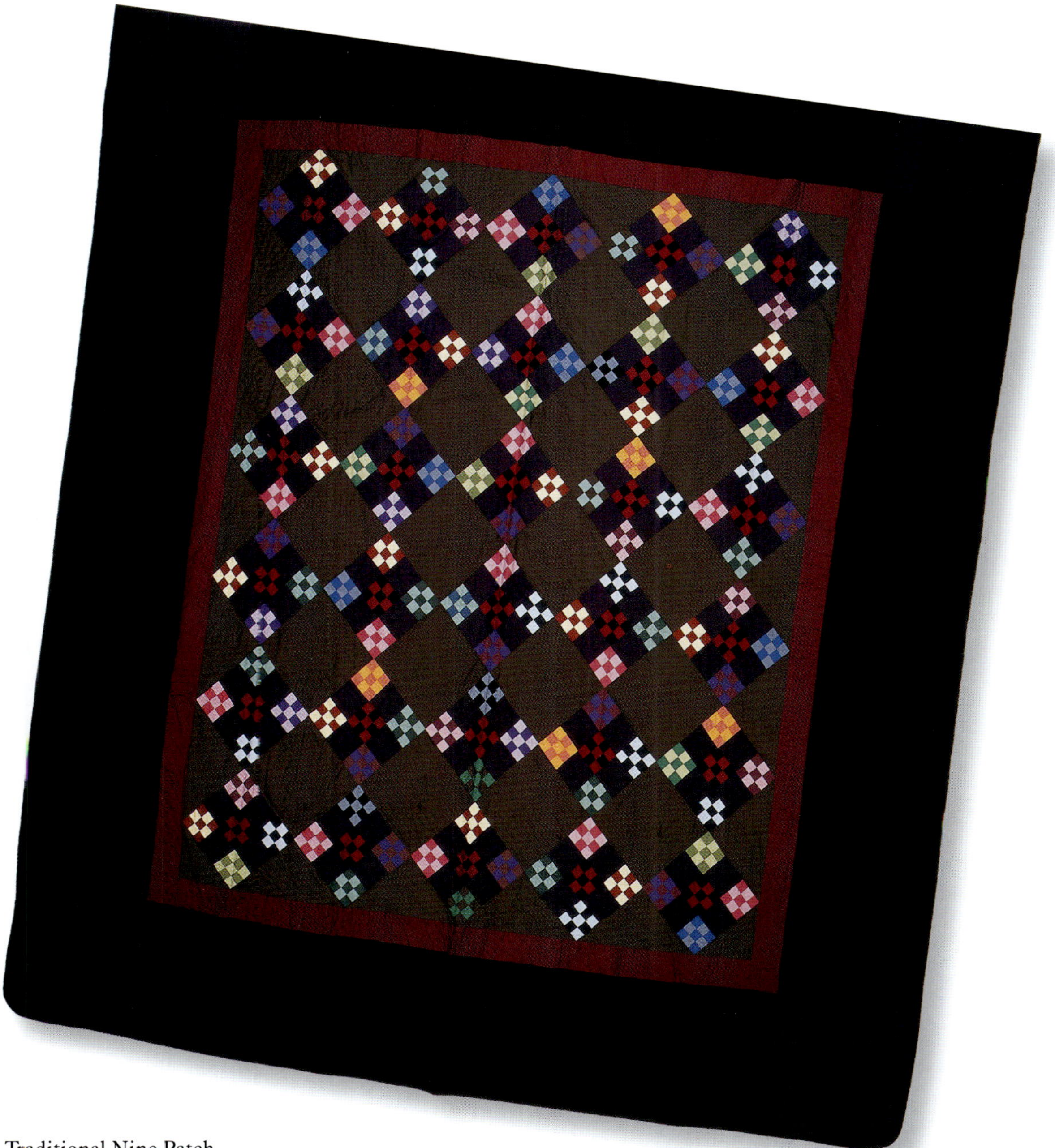

Traditional Nine Patch
Made with traditional Amish colors in solid fabrics and quilted in black thread, Nine Patch fabrics are representative of when fabrics were hand dyed and scraps from clothing were used to bring colors to the quilt.

Double Nine Patch
Made with Amish traditional colors, this wall hanging is a great example of Amish traditional quilting.

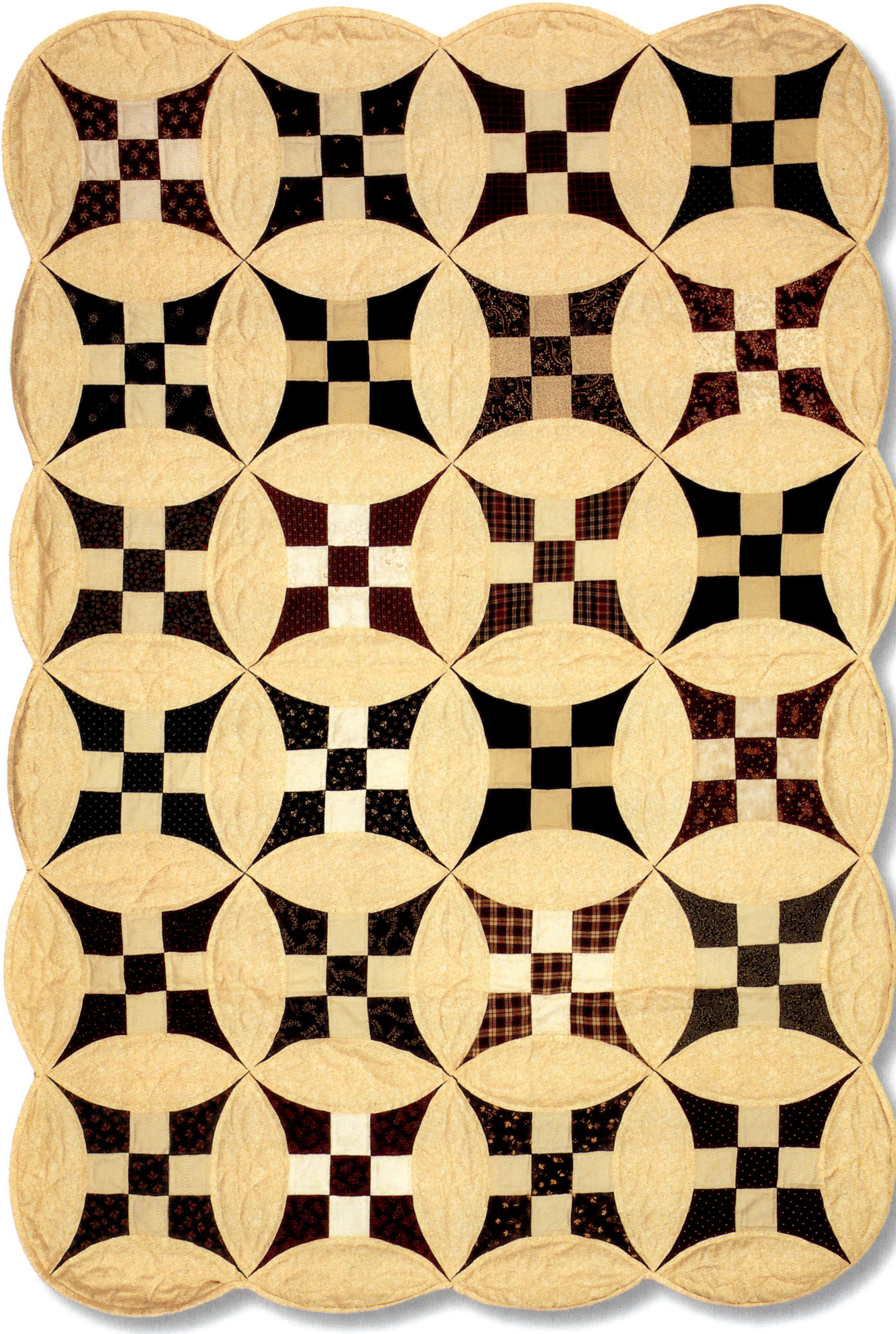

Improved Nine Patch
A modern take on an old pattern, creating a second illusion of a circular element at the union of the patches by adding contour to the traditional Nine Patch pattern.

1930s Reproduction Fabrics

The reproduction fabrics were designed to represent feed sacks from the years of America's great economic Depression. During the Depression, the feed mills would print their fabrics with bright and cheery designs as well as juvenile themed prints to encourage the customers to purchase their products. The sacks were then used to make clothing as well as quilts; original feedsacks are very collectible today. Some collectors make crafts with them, and others collect them by feed brand labels.

Star and Nine Patch
Two traditional Amish patterns combined together, the Amish Eight Point Star and the Nine Patch, and made of 1930s reproduction fabrics.

Heart and Nine Patch
A combination piece and appliqué quilt, a great representation of the 1930s reproduction fabrics that were based on feed sacks.

To the Nines
A modern take on the traditional Nine Patch design made of antique fabrics and highlighted with a marbled navy fabric.

Back Roads of Virginia
A variation of a traditional Nine Patch made with classic burgundy, navy, and green.

Chain or Block Patterns

There are a lot of basic chain or block patterns present in Amish Quilt patterns. From large squares like the Center Diamonds to the smaller blocks like the Irish Chain and Nine Patches, each is simply beautiful as one block and remarkable when set side by side to create a chain. As imagination and talent collide, some beautiful variations to the basic patterns are born.

Weaver Fever
The pattern appears to have a basket weave appearance with many different color waves.

Weaver Fever
Navy, burgundy, and gold enhance the Basket Weave design, which is made of hundreds of small pieces.

Tumbling Block
This Amish traditional pattern is often used to make a multi-dimensional optical illusion. This example is designed with blue, pink, and yellow cubes.

Boston Commons with Appliqué
The use of piecing and appliquéing brought together not only gives an updated look but also softens the look of a pieced quilt.

Jewel Box
This is a good example of a Chain and Block styled quilt. The jewel tone fabrics used in this quilt are mostly boutiques dyed fabrics. Its bright and high contrast colors make this quilt vibrant.

Garden Twist
A great pattern to highlight floral themed fabric and appears to make a lattice design. Each block is enhanced by the hand-quilted patterns stitched into the quilt. The scalloped border is a trademark of this quilter.

Corner of the Garden Twist quilt.

Rachel Lantz signature patch.

Burgoyne Surrounded
A pattern named after a British general's battle formation, this two-color quilt remains a symbol for revolutionary quilts.

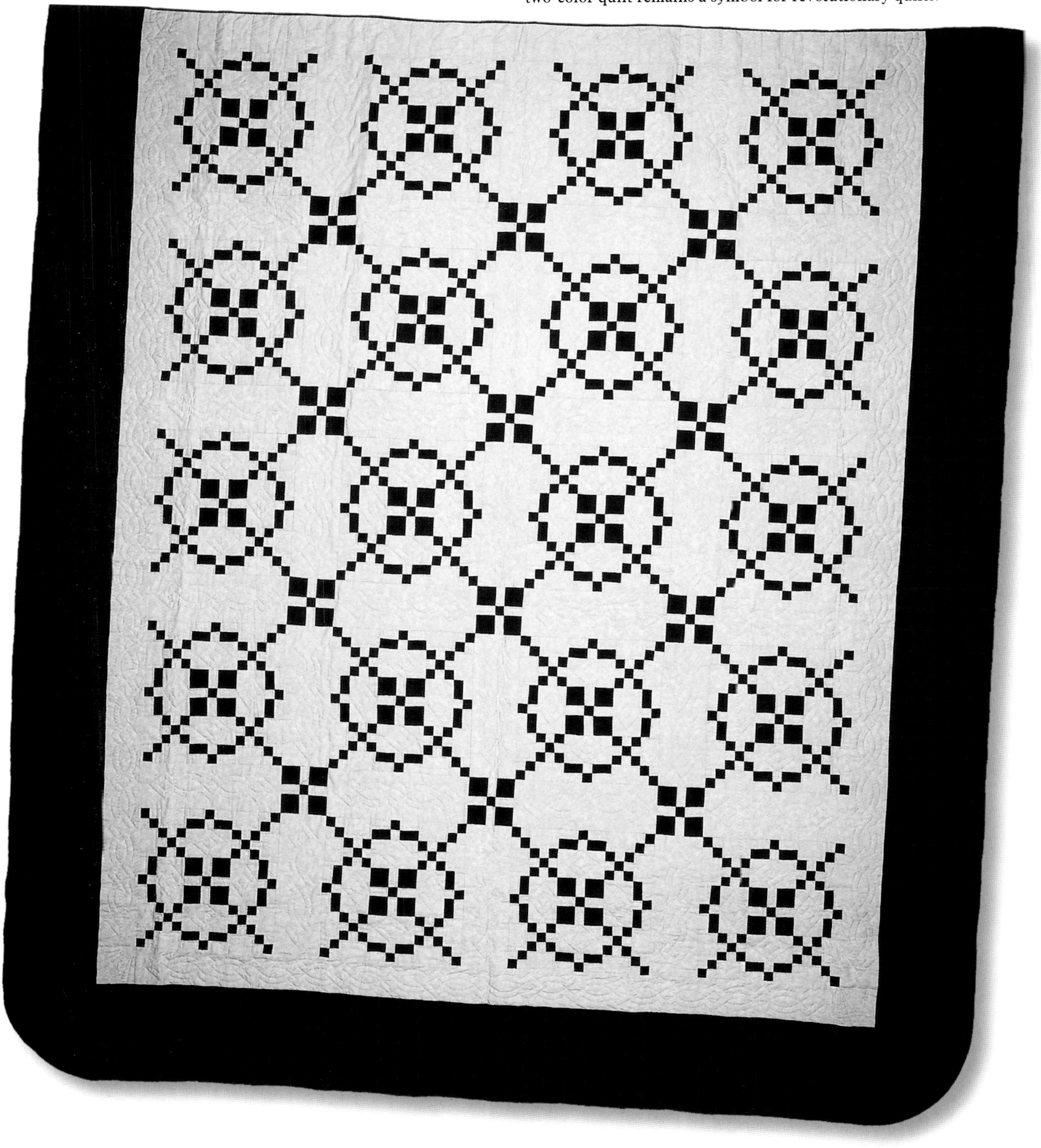

Goose Chase
A version of the Flying Geese pattern, we have adapted the design into a criss-crossing format. Various uses of this pattern have been added to art quilts to add movement to the design. I wonder how many patterns have been made from the original Flying Geese pattern?

Greek Cross
This wall hanging is a good example of a Chain and Block quilt. Even though all Nine Patches are the same, it appears to make a connective sub-pattern.

Richmond
A nine inch block created to make a bar pattern, highlighted with a border fabric colored in poppy red, sage, and coral.

Friends Forever
Made of cotton flannels, this connected block pattern makes a cozy country quilt.

Hovering Hawk
This quilt is a good example of a block quilt. This pattern is beautiful as a single square or set side by side to make a chain.

Hovering Hawk
This coral, sage, and yellow sofa sized quilt can be hung over a couch or on a wall as an accent to a room.

Mosaic Block
A block pattern set up in Nine Patches, with coral, sage, and tan fabrics, combine to make this delightful quilt.

Indian Hatches
The leftover corners of the Mosaic Block pattern were used to make the Indian Hatches quilt.

Lady of the Lake
An old traditional pattern updated by the use of toile prints and gradating color flow.

Snails Trail
This is a traditional pattern that, when set up in a two-color format, exemplifies the movement of this design.

Tilted Pinwheels
This is a modern adaptation of the traditional Pinwheel pattern; bright red, blue, and yellow fabrics are excellent choices for this pattern.

Star Trellis Rose
A derivative of the popular Star patterns, the set up of this quilt creates a secondary trellis theme.

Cathedral Windows
This is an old pattern using a folding technique to make the background; a highlighted fabric is chosen to create the cathedral window. This example is a table runner.

Cathedral Windows
Here is another example of a Cathedral Window.

Jacob's Soul Dance
This quilt is a modern rendition of a traditional Amish pattern called Jacob's Ladder. Add a great imagination and some awesome fabrics and you get a quilt like nothing Grandma has ever seen. The use of border patterns and floral elements will someday become outdated, but today they are used to enhance the design by many quilt artists. I love to use border fabrics when we can; it will be fun to look back years from now and see them.

This two-color patch quilt is done in a classic blue and white, a great example of a Block and Chain quilt.

Here is a popular red and white two-color quilt, a favorite of the early American quilt styles.

Whole Cloth Quilts

Whole cloth quilts are unique in that the pattern is done all in the quilting. This quilt type is made of a whole piece of fabric with no seams. The pattern is marked by using a stencil or by free hand on and then hand quilted. They are usually made with white or off white muslin. What I understand about antique whole cloth from Lancaster County is that because of the availability to wide width fabrics from the fabric mills in the Philadelphia area, these quilts were much more prominent in this area than in other Plain communities.

Miniature whole cloth quilt

Miniature whole cloth quilt.

Hershey's Reproduction

During the Depression, Milton Hershey of Hershey Foods had a whole cloth quilt commissioned for his wife. This is the pattern that was made for her. We now call it "Hershey's Reproduction." It has close to 1000 yards of hand quilting in it. I have been told that the pattern was seen prior to the one commissioned for Mrs. Hershey, but was made more popular by this commissioning.

Hershey's Reproduction Quilt
A medallion whole cloth quilt set on unbleached muslin.

Hershey's Reproduction Quilt

Close up of the Hershey's quilted cable.

Close up of the Hershey's center design.

Pineapple Whole Cloth

This whole cloth quilt was inspired by the Williamsburg motif. The pattern is set up in a circular design. It highlights pineapples, birds, and flowers, all symbols of welcome.

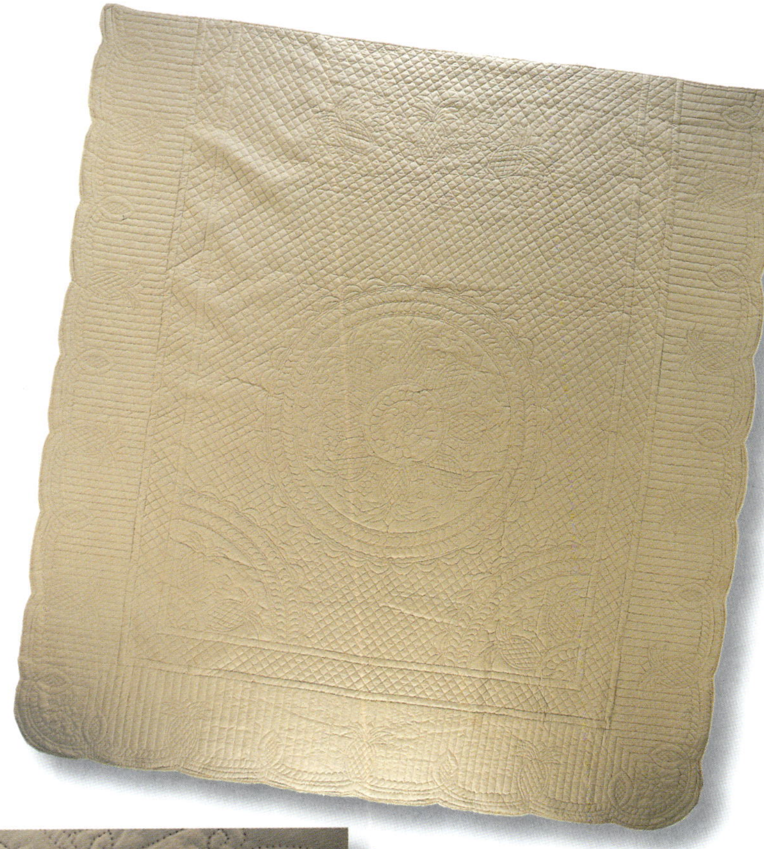

Pineapple quilt.

Close up of the center of the Pineapple quilt.

Round wall hanging of Pineapple whole cloth design.

Close up of the pillow design of the Pineapple quilt.

Close up of hand quilting.

Appliqué

Appliqué quilts have been present in Lancaster County for many years and often depict topics from nature. From basic flowers, trees, and leaves to birds, bears, and snowmen, most appliqué quilts feature art from nature's beauty. Before wide width fabrics were available, appliqué quilts were set up in blocks that would be sewn together after each block was appliquéd. Now we have wide width fabric that the pattern can be applied directly to the large piece of fabric without any blocks required. Whether block style or wide width, both appliqué quilts are very pictorial and eloquent.

Traditional Set Up Appliqué

Whig Rose
This is a traditional block style appliquéd quilt. The quilter, Loraine Zimmerman, is a purist around here; she chooses to do all the quilting steps by hand. Her quilts are hand appliquéd and hand quilted; she goes around the appliqué with a hand buttonhole stitch to accent each piece.

Jacobean Rhapsody
This pattern was derived from an antique crewelwork; with bright fabrics set on black, this is another great example of Lorainne Zimmerman's work.

Close up of the Jacobean Rhapsody quilt.

Close up of a single patch of the Jacobean Rhapsody quilt.

Close up of a single patch of the Jacobean Rhapsody quilt.

Loraine Zimmerman's signature patch on the Jacobean Rhapsody quilt.

Harrison Rose
Derived from the traditional Mennonite appliqué in rose, natural white, and blue. Sometimes there is no need to change anything. That is what I think about this pattern. It has been around for years and still is as beautiful as always.

Harrison Rose
Comprised of burgundy, gold, and sage green fabrics highlighted with detailed quilting.

Close up of Harrison Rose's burgundy, sage, and gold fabrics.

Miniature
This block form is a smaller rendition of the larger pattern. Accented with coral, sage, and butter yellow, is this beautiful example of

Close up from the miniature Rose of Sharon quilt.

Corner of a miniature Rose of Sharon quilt.

Love Dove
Often used as a wedding quilt, this is a hand appliqué, hand quilted design derived from a popular hex sign representing love and prosperity. This quilt is enhanced by its detailed appliqué set up into nine squares.

Lancaster Rose detail.

Appliquéd Sampler
Thirteen different patches bring together the best of Lancaster County appliqué in one creation.

Windy Tulip detail.

Pennsylvania Tulip detail.

Heart Warmer detail.

Center Designed and Wide Width Appliqué

Dogwood in Blossoms
The availability of wide width, tone on tone fabric is a new quilting form and has been a great improvement for appliqué. Although it is a lap full of fabric to deal with, having one piece of fabric for the front makes for a free flowing appliqué design. This Dogwood quilt is a remarkable quilt. The many details, like the individual pieces of fabric that make up the tips to each flower and the twisted bow, all are enhanced by the many yards of hand quilting.

Close up of Dogwood in Blossoms.

Hearts Bouquet
This wall hanging highlights the center pattern of a full sized quilt pattern and is done in lavender and yellows, which create a soft Victorian feel.

Hearts Bouquet
An appliquéd pattern is centralized on top of the bed to give a pictorial feel. This quilt has a lot of appliqué, as well as many hundreds of yards of quilting. It is made with burgundy, rose, and hunter green fabrics to create a Victorian flair.

Close up corner of the Hearts Bouquet quilt.

Close up of center appliqué of the Hearts Bouquet quilt.

Country Love
This pattern is a local Lancaster County design and has been a very popular appliquéd quilt. Its use of cabbage roses makes it different then many other rose patterned quilts.

Grandmother's Wedding Ring
A rendition of Grandmother's Flower Garden, this quilter has chosen to use smaller flowers and piece them together in a ring design. What a great way to use an old pattern and make it fit a new look.

Appliqué and Pieced Applications

Spring Flower in Commons
Combining pieced and appliqué together is a newer idea. This quilt is very effective and is a combination of two popular patterns, the Spring Flower and the Boston Commons.

Floral Festival
This beautiful wall hanging is a combination of hand appliqué and piecework, giving a colonial classic feel. The quilt artist, Karol Umble, is very good with color and her work has a certain look that is easily identifiable as hers.

Karol Umble's signature patch.

Folklore Star
This wall hanging shows the progression of quilts. This is both a pieced and appliquéd quilt using versions of Center Diamond and Mariner's Compass; by combining both methods of quilt making and combining traditional designs, a new look has evolved. It definitely shows the diversity of the quilter's skills and techniques, while also making a very pictorial wall quilt.

Grandmother's Flower Garden
The person that said, "Patience is a virtue" must have made a Grandmother's Flower Garden quilt. This quilt is completely handmade. Each little hexagon is hand sewn together and then hand appliquéd to the background fabric. Various shades of pastel in this wall hanging add to the floral design.

Beauty Everlasting
This quilt is intricate, featuring an appliqué design with a Center Diamond structure complimented by Mariner's Compasses in the corners. This Beauty Everlasting quilt is old fashioned in color with symbolism of rebirth after the Civil War.

Signature patch by Margaret Tulber.

Promises
This deep burgundy and sage green appliqué and patchwork quilt is a great way to have both a strongly colored quilt while having the intricacy of appliqué. I have been told that the plants represented in this quilt were symbols used by the American Indians when making a promise.

Close up of the Promises quilt design.

Mischief
A hand appliquéd wall hanging depicting a cat looking at a bird sitting on a birdhouse.

Kitchen Kettle Quilt
Custom wall hanging created for Kitchen Kettle Village.

Mildred Mast: Collection of Miniature Wall Hangings

Classic folk art is Mildred's specialty. Each piece she makes is different but each holds a look that can easy be identified as a Mildred Mast piece. Whether she was piecing or has appliquéd, every creation has timeless aura about it.

Crows.

Wandering Geese
This miniature quilt's pattern is derived from the traditional Flying Geese pattern.

Rose bud swag.

Flower patch.

Duponi Silk Quilts

Traditionally Lancaster County quilts have been made out of wool and cotton fabrics since they were typical household materials. As we have challenged ourselves to create new quilting patterns, new fabrics have been adopted outside the traditional realm. This quilter has chosen to use Duponi silk and cotton sateen to create a formal appearance to her wall art. New challenges arise when using the Duponi silk due to its delicate nature. Piecing and quilting must be done with great accuracy because you can only pierce the fabric once.

Four Patch
Duponi silk wall hanging.

Large Diamond Patchwork
Duponi silk wall hanging.

Amish Bars in Duponi Silk
This traditional Amish pattern is highlighted, with a center design giving it a modern but formal feel.

A combination of Kaleidoscope and Log Cabin, fabrics are made of Duponi silk and cotton sateen. Champaign, black, and burgundy create this striking piece of wall art.

Two By Four
Made of a combination of cotton sateen and Duponi silk, red, black and gold create an oriental feel.

A great addition to a miniature quilt collections, this patch quilt made of cotton sateen and Duponi silk.

Triple Patch Duponi Silk Wall Hanging
This Duponi silk wall hanging is accented with orange colored silk and highlighted with cotton sateen, bringing a modern but formal appearance to this piece.

Close up of Duponi silk wall hanging.

Jane Crowe Collector Pillows

The passion of quilting is evident in Jane. Over the years Jane has made small quilts, miniature doll beds with quilts on them, and limited edition pillows and collector's Christmas ornaments. One thing that always remains in everything Jane does is her love of 1850s to early 1900s era patterns and colors.

As her collector group has grown, so have her groupings of limited edition collector pillows. We currently have four large groups as well as individual, specialized pillows.

Lancaster County Heritage Set

The Quilt Shop
Of course my favorite pillow in the Lancaster County Heritage Set resembles the Village Quilts building in Intercourse, Pennsylvania. There is so much detail you will definitely not see it all the first time you look at this piece.

Lancaster County Barn
Now this is a familiar scene as you drive into our county. This is the most popular pillow in the series. While each barn is a little different, in colors or season, each resembles local architecture. This unique aspect of her work is one of the great things about collecting her pillows.

Saltbox House
This type of little red brick house is home to many Lancaster County families.

Neighbors
This is one of the latest additions to the Lancaster County series.

Pillows
Red and white patchwork. Set of three.

Pillows
Set of three country patchwork pillows made with burgundy, green, reds, and gold.

Pillows
Set of three pillows comprised of Americana checkerboards.

Pillows
Americana themed pillows, My Country, My Liberty, Mini Flag, and Star ornament.

Jane Crow signature patch.

Stuffed Animals

This bear is made out of a Grandmother's Flower Garden quilt from the 1930s, a wonderful way to enable quilts to continue on in a new form. Our quilt artists disassemble old quilts that are in need of some recycling and make them live on through these creations.

Star
This was made from a few different antique quilts and accented with vintage buttons.

Mouse
Doesn't he look like he has a story to tell? The mouse was made from a hand-pieced vintage Grandmother's Fan quilt.

Pastel Teddy Bear
Another creation made out of recycled antique quilts. This was probably a baby blanket in its first life.

A rabbit made from a vintage quilt.

Wearable Arts

Textile Art Jacket 2005-2006 Crazy Patch Edition

At Village Quilts, each winter the staff chooses a project to work on. The jackets have been favorites of many of our guest. As of this edition, there were over eighty jackets made. Each year the look and style changes, so they have become very collectable.

Crazy Quilt Edition: this jacket's colors are royal blue, lime green, and yellow, accented with a beautiful butterfly motif.

Signature blocks and Village Quilts tags from a quilted jacket.

Textile Art Jacket 2005-2006, Crazy Patch edition: this jacket has an Oriental theme.

This jacket has a country French feel, highlighting the bright blues and yellow hues. This jacket is sure to get noticed at any festivities. The theme fabric is a brightly colored butterfly, highlighted by coordinating crazy patch pieces.

Textile Art Jacket 2005-2006 Crazy Patch edition: highlighted with a beautiful floral fabrics in various shades of lavender.

Textile Art Jacket 2005-2006 Crazy Patch edition: themed fabric printed with ornate Chinese vase. This jacket can be worn with many different outfits.

Tote Bags

Due to the passion for all things quilted, quilt-themed bags have become popular items for the quilt artist as well as the quilt enthusiasts.

Center Diamond Tote Bag: this bag features the traditional Amish motif.

Log Cabin Tote Bag: pattern highlighting a floral pattern highlighted in blue, burgundy, and rose.

Center Diamond Tote Bag: highlighting an Oriental fabric.

Log Cabin Tote Bag: features a variety of pastel prints.